Countries

Mexico

by Christine Juarez

raintree
a Capstone company — publishers for children

Raintree is an imprint of Capstone Global Library Limited, a company incorporated in England and Wales having its registered office at 264 Banbury Road, Oxford, OX2 7DY – Registered company number: 6695582

www.raintree.co.uk
myorders@raintree.co.uk

Edited by Erika L. Shores
Designed by Bobbie Nuytten
Picture research by Wanda Winch
Production by Jennifer Walker

Printed in China
ISBN 978 1 4747 1982 7
20 19 18 17 16
10 9 8 7 6 5 4 3 2 1

British Library Cataloguing in Publication Data
A full catalogue record for this book is available from the British Library.

Photo Credits
Capstone, 4, 22 (currency); Corbis: Royalty-Free, 19; Dreamstime: Jerl71, 15, Richard Gunion, 17; Shutterstock: Eduardo Rivero, 9, f9photos, 21, Frontpage, 5, Joao Virissimo, cover, Matty Symons, 1,7, Melaics, cover, 1 (design element), movit, 22 (flag), Ohmega1982, back cover globe, Sumikophoto, 13, tipograffias, 11

We would like to thank Gail Saunders-Smith, Ph.D., for her invaluable help in the preparation of this book.

Every effort has been made to contact copyright holders of material reproduced in this book. Any omissions will be rectified in subsequent printings if notice is given to the publisher.

All the internet addresses (URLs) given in this book were valid at the time of going to press. However, due to the dynamic nature of the internet, some addresses may have changed, or sites may have changed or ceased to exist since publication. While the author and publisher regret any inconvenience this may cause readers, no responsibility for any such changes can be accepted by either the author or the publisher.

Note to Parents and Teachers

The Countries series supports learning related to people, places and culture. This book describes and illustrates Mexico. The images support early readers in understanding the text. The repetition of words and phrases helps early readers learn new words. This book also introduces early readers to subject-specific vocabulary, which is defined in the Glossary section. Early readers may need assistance to read some words and to use the Contents, Glossary, Read more, Websites and Index sections of the book.

Contents

Where is Mexico?

Mexico is a country in North America. Mexico is south of the United States. The capital of Mexico is Mexico City.

MEXICO

Mexico City

Landforms and climate

Sandy beaches line Mexico's coasts. Mexico also has deserts, rainforests and mountains. The weather in Mexico is usually warm and dry.

Animals

Many kinds of animals live in
Mexico. Golden eagles nest
in trees. Toucans live in
Mexico's rainforests. Coyotes live
in the deserts and mountains.

Language and population

More than 116 million people live in Mexico. Most Mexicans live in cities. Spanish is the country's official language.

11

Food

Many Mexicans buy their food at open air markets. They buy chilli peppers, bananas and beans. People enjoy tortillas, tacos and rice.

Celebrations

Mexicans celebrate the Day of the Dead. This holiday is in November. Families visit the graves of their loved ones. They bring flowers and food.

Where people work

Many Mexicans have jobs to do with tourism. Other Mexicans work in shops and factories. Farmers grow wheat, coffee, cotton, corn and fruit.

Transportation

Many Mexicans travel by car or by bus. In cities, taxis are busy, too. In the mountains, people ride horses.

CIRCUITO INTERIOR ↑
← CHAPULTEPEC

Famous sight

Thousands of years ago, people in Mexico built huge, stone pyramids. Some pyramids are still standing. Visitors climb many steps to reach the tops of the pyramids.

Country facts

Name: United Mexican States

Capital: Mexico City

Population: 116,220,947 (July 2013 estimate)

Size: 1,964,375 square kilometres (758,449.43 square miles)

Language: Spanish

Main crops: corn, wheat, rice, beans, coffee, fruit

Mexico's flag

Money: Mexican peso

Glossary

capital city in a country where the government is based

chilli pepper small, spicy food used to flavour spicy sauces

coast land next to an ocean or sea

desert very dry area of land

factory place where a product, such as a car, is made

grave place where a dead person is buried

language words used in a particular country or by a particular group of people

North America continent that includes the United States, Canada, Mexico and Central America

official having the approval of a country or a certain group of people

pyramid structure that is big at the bottom and small at the top; many of the pyramids in Mexico have steps

rainforest tropical forest where a lot of rain falls

tortilla round, flat bread

tourism business of taking care of visitors when they travel to a different country or place

Read more

Introducing North America (Introducing Continents), Chris Oxlade (Raintree, 2014)

Mexico: A Benjamin Blog and His Inquisitive Dog Guide (Country Guides), Anita Ganeri (Raintree, 2015)

Websites

ngkids.co.uk/places/country-fact-file-mexico

Explore facts about Mexico's culture, history, geography and more.

www.timeforkids.com/destination/mexico

Learn about the history of Mexico and other facts on this website.

Index